PRODUCT STRATEGY & ROADMAPS

Linda Gorchels

Copyright © 2021, 2017 Linda Gorchels

All rights reserved.,

No part of this publication may be reproduced, distributed, or transmitted in any form or by any means, including photocopying, recording, or other electronic or mechanical methods, without the prior written permission of the author, except in the case of brief quotations embodied in critical reviews and certain other noncommercial uses permitted by copyright law.

Cover Photo by Anna Shvets from Pexels.

Table of Contents

Preface

Chapter One: Business as usual?
- Are we on the same page?
- Strategy requires vision
- How to begin
  - Example product vision statements
  - From vision to concept
- Should you be first to market?

Chapter Two: Define a growth agenda
- Product growth arenas
  - Sustaining Growth
  - Transformative Growth
  - Disruptive Growth

Chapter Three: Platform strategy
- Technology vs. product platforms
  - Pros and cons of product platforms
  - The architecture of product platforms

Chapter Four: Roadmapping
- Envision a collectively identified future
- Creating the roadmap

Chapter Five: Product market research

- The research pyramid
- Common research dichotomies
- Tools, methods and techniques

Chapter Six: Self-reflection
- Suggested references
  - Product Vision
  - Growth Strategies
  - Product Platforms and Roadmaps
  - Product Market Research

About the Author

Books in the ShortRead Series
- Product Management 101
- Product Strategy & Roadmaps

Books by this Author
- The Product Manager's Handbook
- Product Management 101
- The Manager's Guide to Distribution Channels
- Business Model Renewal

Preface

In the first ShortRead book (Product Management 101), I stated that product literacy is a must-have aptitude for product managers. Seems pretty obvious. But is it?

Product + literacy. It's a person's knowledge about a particular product. But there's more. It's the ability to communicate with diverse others about it. It encompasses vision, strategy, planning and roadmapping. That's the focus of this volume of the ShortRead Series.

This is not a book on new products per se. It's about the strategy at the "fuzzy front end," the thinking and foresight to prepare for the future. It precedes and guides development through goals, strategies, and iterative research.

Chapter One: Business as usual?

Do the following news items suggest the end of business as usual?

*The Craftsman Tools imprint was almost synonymous with Sears since 1927. It has been an iconic brand. Its famous replacement warranty, until 2012, was lifetime and unlimited. Things have changed. Sears sold the Craftsman line to Stanley Black & Decker for $900 million in 2017.

*Borders, an international book and music retail chain, opened business in 1971. By 2010 it operated 511 superstores and had nearly 20,000 employees. It filed for bankruptcy in 2011, having not made a profit since 2006.

*Amazon has opened physical bookstores in at least twelve states plus the District of Columbia. They also have stores with highly curated merchandise (Amazon 4-star), along with food stores (Amazon Fresh, Amazon Go, and Amazon Go Grocery).

*There was a time when BlackBerry was king of the mobile market, before iPhones and Android products. Its first mobile phone was the "darling of Corporate America." But it didn't maintain its position in a touchscreen world.

*Buying light bulbs used to be pretty simple. You chose which wattage of incandescent bulb you wanted and pulled out your credit card (or cash). Then the ecosystem changed with new lighting standards that took effect in 2012. Production of incandescent bulbs has phased out, being replaced by a host of alternatives including halogen incandescent, compact fluorescents (CFL) and light-emitting diode (LED) bulbs. Each of these has sub-categories.

*Driverless vehicles, electric cars, and delivery drones are just a few products that could be game changers in industry.

Each of these examples suggested a beginning or an end of a product line, sometimes simultaneously. But do they signify the end of business as we know it? Many industries and products have indeed become obsolete. But companies continue to succeed and fail, innovate and degenerate, grow and decline. Is there a "secret" to success? Is it the business model… or the strategy… or the leadership… or the products… or just being at the right place at the right time?

Obviously, all these factors play a role. Or stated more accurately, the factors play different roles under different circumstances. As a product manager, think about these big picture issues as you contemplate your product goals and strategies. But before I jump into that, let's define a few terms.

Are we on the same page?

Listen to people define terms related to strategy. Even within the same company, what one calls a business model another calls a strategy. Someone else refers to a strategy as a tactic. A vision flipflops with a mission statement, as does leadership and management. There are no foolproof definitions. Managers use the terms inconsistently. Problems arise when different definitions cause a breakdown in communication, or create avoidable misinterpretations.

Here are the definitions I use. It's a starting point.

Business model   How a firm produces value—including strategy, organizational design, infrastructure, culture and organizational processes. It's comprehensive. The business model may contain a company vision statement that's an umbrella over visions of the products it offers. The company and product visions foster a shared understanding of the direction to plot for the future.

Product vision   A fuzzy representation of a future state—what the product *aspires* to become. It is a theme, a direction for an individual product, a platform, or a portfolio. It is indistinct (yet comprehensible). Product managers can't divorce the vision from competencies inherent in the business model.

Product concept   A semi-concrete product description that flows from the vision statement. It contains sufficient market and operational data to drive iterations, business case and development efforts.

Goal   The desired business result (the long-term *what*) of a strategic plan. We could state it as future sales of a new product, long-term entries into new markets with existing products, or other future outcomes.

Strategy	A long-term plan of action (the long-term *how*) to achieve a goal. From a military perspective, strategy is the plan to win the war, while tactics are the actions taken to win a battle. A product strategy comprises multi-year efforts to attain business results.
Objective	The desired business result (the short-term what) of a short-term plan to move toward the long-term vision and goals. An objective is more specific and concretely measurable than a goal. It links annual plans with long-term strategic plans. It answers the question: what am I going to accomplish this year to move closer to the long-term goal from where I am right now? What will be the sales revenue, units, profits of the portfolio of products this fiscal year?
Tactic	A short-term action or activity (the short-term how) to achieve an objective. Some tactics are proactive. Others are reactive, addressing internal or external realities that might not have been clear or present when you developed the strategy.

Goal	=	**Long-term what**
Strategy	=	**Long-term how**
Objective	=	**Short-term what**
Tactic	=	**Short-term how**

STRATEGY REQUIRES VISION

There is a reason I defined the terms. As I mentioned above, a strategy is a plan of action, whereas a goal results from that plan. Strategies have more flexibility than goals. In fact, an overemphasis on a defined strategy can sometimes obstruct the attainment of the goal. Here is an analogy. When my kids were little, my husband and I had a *vision* of taking unique and educational summer trips with our children. A *goal* spawned by this vision was a trip to the Grand Canyon. Since we live just a few hours north of Chicago, we took Route 66 as a nostalgic tour through old America (our *strategy*). This historic highway spawned a TV show in the 1960s (*Route 66*) and received lyrical tributes ("get their kicks on Route 66"). Unfortunately, we discovered that Route 66 no longer existed in its entirety, sometimes merging with other roadways and at other times stopping completely. (The government decommissioned it in the 1980s.)

The actual *strategy* of driving on Route 66 yielded new information. Each day resulted in a new driving plan to recalibrate our efforts. While the *vision* (educational trips) and strategic *goal* (driving to the Grand Canyon) were mostly consistent and stable, the implementation plans for the strategy were more dynamic. But note this. If we had continued solely with Route 66 (the strategy), we never would have arrived at the Grand Canyon (our goal)!

I have experienced this phenomenon with several clients. They may continue pursuing a particular customer acquisition approach, a product-development effort, or a cost-cutting measure long after it has deviated from the goal. They (often unconsciously) place fulfillment of the strategy above the attainment of the goal. While staying true to a strategy that requires goal modification is sometimes the correct approach, it's not the norm. It's more likely that you should stay true to the goal and change your approach to achieve it.

Coming up with the right goal is a significant predecessor to strategy.

I'm not saying that visions and goals alone will make strategies happen. Their reason for being is to provide direction. But simply claiming that a goal **is** the strategy doesn't work either. We've all heard politicians make statements such as "*my strategy is to create jobs*" or "*my plan is to balance the budget.*" Those aren't strategies or plans. They're goals (or perhaps platitudes). They're relatively meaningless without some inclusion of the *how* of strategy. Goals provide the direction (the *what*); strategies provide the *how*. Vision provides the *why*, the aspirational, motivational component of strategic planning.

How to Begin

Okay. If everything starts with the vision, how do you create it?

Look for an opportunity in the marketplace. Identify a strength to solve it. Sounds simple, huh?

The vision describes a solution to a shortcoming—or a closing of a gap—in the marketplace. But that's only half of it. You must also determine the competencies, capabilities and resources of the individual or organization required to make it happen. Before I wrote the first edition of The Product Manager's Handbook (early 1990s), I tried to find books and resources to use in my product management training. Few existed. Given the gap in educational resources, I wondered whether I could partner with a publisher to develop a product that would fit. My (yet unfocused) vision was to produce a resource to use for training and follow up.

As is true of all visions, this one was fuzzy at first. My customers were asking for a resource they could use outside the workshop. They wanted something practical rather than academic. Yet they didn't want an "opinion" piece—it needed to be grounded in research of what was out there. I understood the gap that existed. Since I had been in product management and in marketing research prior to joining the university, I felt I had some—but not all—of the competencies to address the needs. The future was still aspirational at this point. I reached out to experts in the field and learned from them. Their suggestions and input led to ongoing motivation to succeed. I signed a contract with a major publisher and the book shifted from vision to product concept to implementation.

The vision for a product can emerge from internal and external sources. Existing products may have visible deficiencies apparent to most of the market. Customers might request specific product attributes companies can extend to a larger market. An accidental discovery can open up a market where none existed.

Companies may require product managers to develop a vision for new products to achieve business growth objectives. That could mean cultivating core products for sustaining growth. Or moving into adjacent markets for transformative growth. Or creating new markets for disruptive growth. I will look at this more fully in chapter two, *Define a Growth Agenda*. Regardless of initial impetus, the product vision must describe an aspirational, motivational, and valuable future. AND, it must be more than a promotional platitude.

Example product vision statements

Product visions can take many forms and are valuable as a trigger for strategy development. Here are a few illustrative product visions.

> *Medical:* to predict impending heart failure, enable proactive patient management, and reduce hospital health-failure readmissions

This statement deals with the challenges of recurrent heart failure. There are over <u>one million heart-failure hospitalizations</u> in the U.S. annually, with 25% readmitted within 30 days of initial admission. Traditional physiologic markers (patient weight, symptoms, and blood pressure) are reactive and inexact. Simultaneously, advances in the ability to collect digital biomarkers have enabled AI-driven data. These trends are the backdrop for the first vision.

There is an obvious market need, and addressing the need can save lives. The vision is motivational and drives the direction of the product concept. How the vision comes to life depends on the product concept. Here is one (hypothetical) example for a concept named WISE.

> WISE is an implantable diagnostic monitoring system with multiple sensors to track physiological trends. It enables a remote alert to be sent to clinicians via a proprietary algorithm, with a low rate of inaccurate signals. The device will advance the field of electrophysiology.

Note that the concept statement addresses the benefits sought in the vision statement. It's not yet a detailed product description. The specific sensors and algorithm are not shared (and perhaps not yet fully developed at the time the concept statement was written). The comment about advancing the field of electrophysiology implies that this will be a novel product in the industry.

I show the relationship between the vision and concept below.

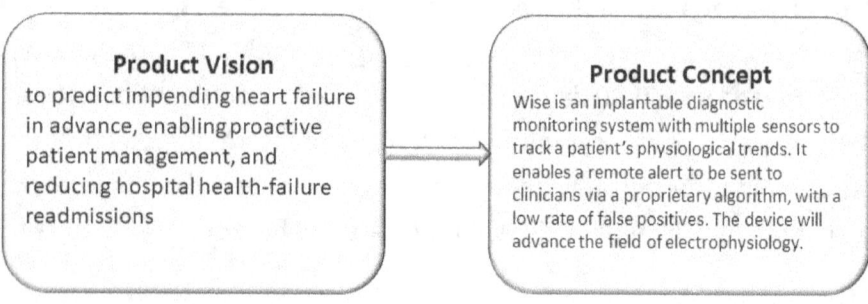

Umbrella consumer product: to innovate personal care products with eco-friendly design, materials, packaging and shipping

This second vision statement is broader, applicable for one product or a family of products. Like the prior example, marketplace problems drive it. In 2018, we landfilled nearly 27 million tons of plastic. Yet, according to The New Plastics Economy report by the Ellen MacArthur Foundation "72% of plastic packaging is not recovered at all." This creates significant negative externalities for oceans, food systems, and people.

Consumer awareness is strong. According to a recent BCG survey, 87% of respondents believed private companies should integrate environmental considerations into their products or services. And some companies have moved in that direction. P&G has a goal of achieving 100% recyclable or reusable packaging by 2030. Nestle made a similar commitment for 2025.

It's clear there are ecosystem, consumer sentiment, and competitive factors driving the vision.

The term *innovate* in the vision prescribes that the resulting product concepts are more than line extensions. Both the core items and their delivery should be environmentally sound. Take toothpaste, for example. Does it need to be a paste or a gel to facilitate brushing teeth? Does it need to be in a single-use tube? Bite toothpaste bits are dry tablets that come in reusable glass jars with compostable refill pouches. The company has a mission of going plastic-free. (Well Earth Goods, Earth Hero and others also offer toothpaste tablets.) A potential product concept could have been: a sustainable and natural toothpaste alternative that can be manufactured, packaged and shipped with no plastics and a minimal environmental footprint. As with the medical example, the concept is not yet a final product description and allows for more details to emerge through the discovery process.

The umbrella vision statement applies to product families or categories. Continuing with the dental care category, the product family concept could include floss, toothbrushes and mouthwash.

The connection between vision and concepts is shown below. Note that the vision states what you are going to do: to predict, to innovate. The concept is a high-level product that achieves the vision.

Umbrella Product Vision
To innovate personal care products with eco-friendly design, materials, packaging and shipping

Product Concept
The product is a sustainable and natural toothpaste alternative that can be manufactured, packaged and shipped with no plastics and minimal environmental footprint.

Product Family Concept
Eco-Dental is a product line including biodegradable floss, bamboo toothbrushes, toothpaste tablets and mouthwash tablets, all manufactured, packaged and shipped with no plastics and minimal environmental footprint.

Platform vision statement

A platform vision statement starts at the end, defining a range of future products that share common elements. Feature sets, price points, and target customers may vary, yet the products build on the same core product architecture. While technology platforms are common today, they aren't the only type of platforms. Later in the book I point out platform examples from the automotive industry ad consumer package goods.

The platform vision comes after you define future derivative products. It starts with the end in mind. Whereas the umbrella product vision in the prior example *allows* for future derivatives, the platform vision *plans* for it.

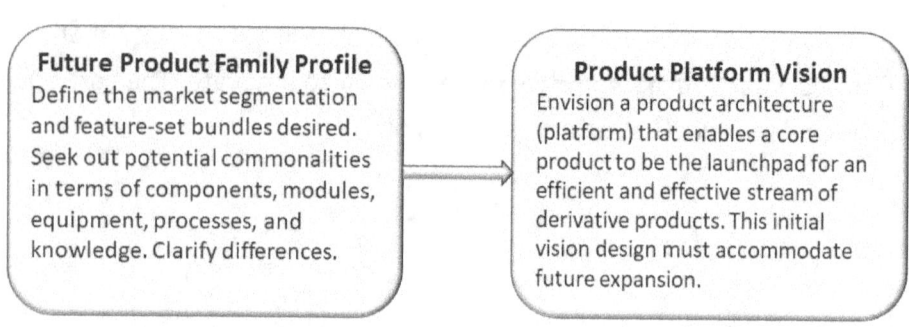

Even though the product vision statements are quite different, in some ways they are the same. They:

*build on a foundation of data

*are future-focused, using terms like *to become, to create,* or *to improve*

*spotlight benefits that are inspirational, or at a minimum, directional

*set the stage for brainstorming product concepts

From vision to concept

Product concepts are descriptions of items arising from brainstorming the benefits specified in the vision. The history of one of 3M's products provides an example of the brainstorming from vision to concept.

In the 1980s, Eric von Hippel worked with what was then the 3M™ Medical Products group on a project to investigate solutions for the decline in antibiotic effectiveness during surgery. In the 3M™ lead user study the researchers conducted primary, secondary and observational research to arrive at a product vision: *"product concepts to dramatically improve microbial control in the surgical settings of today and tomorrow with significantly reduced costs."*

The vision focused on a gap in the marketplace, identified through various data collection methods and proprietary knowledge. The goal was to create products that would dramatically improve microbial control and improve on the existing Ioban™ incise drape design. (The history of the continued innovation on the 3M™ Ioban™ Antimicrobial Incise Drapes is on the 3M website.)

They then brought lead users into a series of workshops to explore ideas. The purpose of the workshops was to describe *"at least three concepts with dynamic elements"* and to identify *"key system elements needed to make the product successful."*

Converting a product vision to a product concept requires looking at the big picture, including what the 3M example referred to as "key system elements needed to make the product successful." The process includes not only the product and customers, but also the business model components required.

You must thoughtfully and objectively answer standard business questions to test the viability of the product concept. Several authors have proposed putting all the relevant information on a one-page canvas. If that works for you, do it! The downside to the approach is that you could miss deeper nuances of the issues.

If you want deeper insights, fill all the whiteboards in your boardroom with answers (and questions) and use sticky notes to prioritize. The downside to this approach is that you could feel overwhelmed with too much data.

Or you could use an old-fashioned SWOT analysis on the concept. What are the strengths and weaknesses of your company as they relate to developing the product? How can you capitalize on the strengths and minimize the weaknesses? What existing opportunities can you leverage? (For example, what market, technology, industry and/or regulatory trends are working in favor of the concept?) What threats pose a risk to success and how will you minimize them? The downside to a SWOT analysis, like the whiteboard approach, is that you can drown in data.

Pick the best pieces from the approaches and use what works for you. Just be sure that somewhere in the process you answer the following questions.

> *What is this thing?*
>
> > Describe what the product is (and what is it isn't). Use verbal descriptions, sketches, mock-ups, models or prototypes. Link the concept to the product vision and the corporate/business strategy.
>
> *Who will be the purchasers of the product?*
>
> > This includes users (buyer personas, perhaps), as well as channels to reach them. It may help to identify influencers and other intermediaries.

What is the competition?

> List products, companies or activities that compete—directly or indirectly—with this proposed product. Take a broad look at competition. Remember, cell phones disrupted the camera industry, Uber disrupted the taxicab industry, and wash-and-wear clothing disrupted the dry-cleaning industry.

Why will customers buy this? What will they pay?

> Not only does the product need to differ from the competition, the difference needs to be valuable. Customers must spend money on it. If you can't monetize the benefits, the value proposition is too weak.

What resources, expertise and costs will product development require?

> Consider all engineering, manufacturing, marketing, and other expenditures. Can you do it with existing resources, or will you need to contract outside the company? Is that possible and realistic?

What assumptions, if wrong, could derail the product.

> Think about market shifts, technological disruptions, and political upheavals. How might they affect this product? How likely are they? What can you do to reduce risk?

SHOULD YOU BE FIRST TO MARKET?

When planning strategy, product managers often want to be first to market. Is that always the best plan?

Who was the first person on the moon? Who was the first person to break the sound barrier? Who was the first woman to fly solo across the Atlantic?

The answers are, in order, Neil Armstrong, Chuck Yeager, and Amelia Earhart.

Who was number two?

Most people can't answer who the second person was in these categories. That fact is often used to justify first mover advantage. It's the most memorable position.

Shift now to business. What was the first MP3 player? What was the first social networking site to connect and share with your family and friends online? What was the first e-book reader?

If you answered iPod, FaceBook and Kindle, you'd be wrong. According to Wikipedia, SaeHan Information Systems developed the first MP3 player in 1997. Diamond MultiMedia, Sony and others sold products prior to the launch of the iPod in 2001. In fact, an [Atlantic article](#) stated there were about 50 MP3 players available then.

Friendster and MySpace preceded FaceBook. The Rocket eBook, launched in 1998, was the first dedicated eBook reader. SoftBook launched the same year, and the Franklin eBookman entered the market in 1999. Amazon released the first Kindle in 2007.

What gives?

There is a misconception that being first to market is always an advantage. Being first to market can work when:

*the new product provides a demonstrable and significant benefit to customers

*it requires minimal buyer behavior change

*competitors are unlikely to one-up you soon

*you've worked out all the potential bugs in the system

There may be logic to launching a product *after* learning from and correcting mistakes of others. People perceive iPod, FaceBook and Kindle as the first *successful* product in each category, even though none were the first movers. Rather, they learned from prior market entrants.

Most product managers are familiar with the concept of the product life cycle. Breakthrough products go through a tumultuous introduction phase. It starts with a low awareness of the product, few competitors and meager growth. There may even be chasms prior to that phase during which growth temporarily stops or declines, as shown in the following visual.

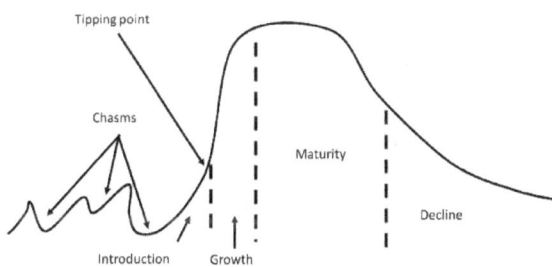

Sales grow slowly during the introduction phase. Then a tipping point occurs when sales accelerate into the growth phase. During this second phase, there are more customers, more competitors, and (hopefully) an increase in profitability. Competition is intense during maturity, forcing companies to focus on differential positioning strategies. Sales decline at the end of the lifecycle, and most products become obsolete. If the market doesn't evaporate entirely, it may plateau with a few remaining products. These few may have healthy profit margins, at least temporarily.

The value of this model is not as a predictive tool, but as an insight tool for *market* growth. Product managers don't control the entire market; they control their own products. Market growth and product growth are not synonymous. It's useful to think about both the stage of the market life cycle (MLC) and the stage of your product life cycle (PLC), as shown in the following chart.

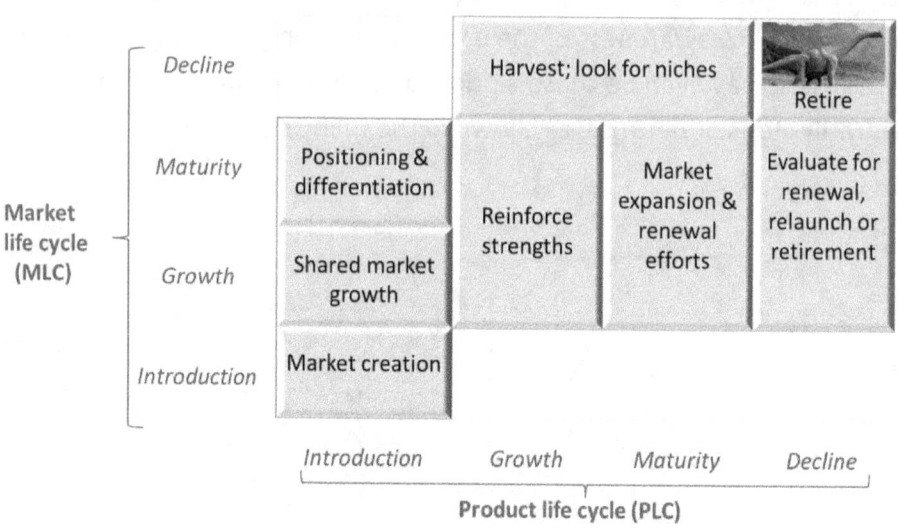

If the product you are launching is *creating a* new market (i.e., both the product lifecycle and the market lifecycle are in the introduction phase), your strategy will need to be one of market creation. You will need to identify innovators and market influencers who can help generate buzz for the new product category. You will face indirect competition initially, and will need to convince prospects to try something new. The more customers have to change their behavior to use a new product, the harder it will be to sell. This is especially true if they don't believe there are dramatic benefits from the new item.

Think about the amount of customer behavior change required in relation to product advantage. The following matrix from John T. Gourville's Harvard Business Review article, *Eager Sellers and Stony Buyers: Understanding the Psychology of New-Product Adoption,* shows this.

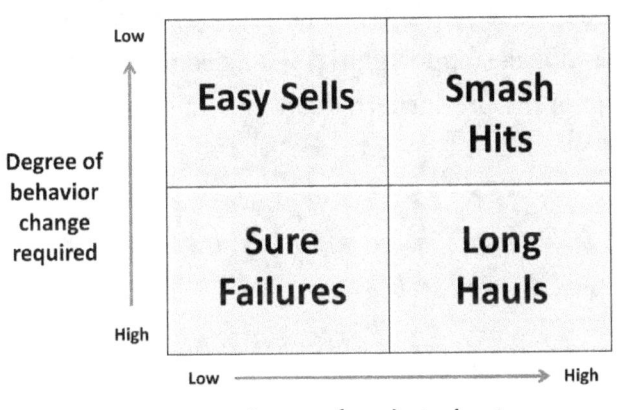

Behavior change can be a hurdle for customers to overcome before they'd consider buying a new product. Buying electric cars requires a change in powering (fueling) the vehicle. The advantage is high, but so is the expected behavior change. To be successful in this product category, you have to be prepared for a long haul. (After decades of slow growth, this product market's potential is speeding up.) Selling a less expensive cell phone with dramatically superior features could be a smash hit.

Keep in mind that customer switching costs can be economic (needing to buy different accessories) or psychological ("I like the way I'm doing things now"). Either way, they're real. Unless product managers take those obstacles into account, they may underestimate the time and effort it will take to achieve goals. After all, we still use QWERTY keyboards, and the United States has not yet adopted the metric system.

If you are launching a product into a growth market, you have the advantage of sharing customer education with your competitors. You may have also learned from the mistakes of early entrants. If you are launching a product into a mature market, positioning and differentiation will be critical. As your product moves from growth to maturity, take cues from *market lifecycle stages* to make decisions. Reposition brand image, reinforce strengths, and look for sales opportunities in adjacent markets. If decline is inevitable, discontinue the product. This can free up resources for new products and services.

Chapter Two: Define a growth agenda

As contradictory as it may seem, there is an opportunity cost to growth. Resources devoted to one product might be better invested in another. Timing of profits poses another conundrum. Is it better to harvest current product for the immediate win or "bet the farm" for huge payouts in the future? The unsatisfactory answer is *it depends*. Not all product managers have the absolute freedom to make this decision. Yet, most have a voice.

Where possible, think in terms of a portfolio of products. Just as future retirees reduce risk through a mix of *safe* and *aggressive* financial offerings, product managers benefit from similar thinking in their product line. Look for opportunities to raise profits from core products to reinvest in growth products for the future.

Be open to marketplace transitions and to customer behavior shifts. How many people now *listen* to books and *read* cell phones. A handful of events like these can change your product strategy in significant ways.

Expand your approach to success by considering multiple prosperity domains, or growth arenas.

PRODUCT GROWTH ARENAS

Revenue and profitability can come from three arenas, as shown in the following figure.

*Sustaining growth by defending and extending core products

*Driving transformative growth by incrementally moving into adjacent products or markets

*Seeding disruptive growth by exploring breakthrough ideas

	Boost existing customer markets	Move into adjacent customer markets	Create new customer markets
Cultivate and reframe existing products, offerings, revenue streams and competencies	**Sustaining Growth Arena** (shorter-term planning horizon; mine the core)		
Cultivate and collaborate with external partners for products, offerings, revenue streams and competencies		**Transformative Growth Arena** (intermediate-term planning horizon; advance into adjacencies)	**Disruptive Growth Arena** (long-term planning horizon; incite breakthroughs)

Note that I used dotted curves that don't connect precisely with row and column nodes. That was by design. There is a lot of gray area between sustaining growth and transformative growth, and between transformative growth and disruptive growth. In the real world, these arenas bleed into each other. That's okay. I want you to use this tool to provoke thinking rather than as a template to complete. Don't force your products and strategies into an arena. Like the product lifecycle, this is not a predictive tool, but an insight tool.

Many authors use different terms to describe these growth strategies. For the first domain, sustaining, incremental and core are common descriptors. While sustaining growth may not sound as sexy or powerful as scrapping your core products and "shooting for the moon," it's important. Be aware that as a product changes over time through a series of incremental innovations, the difference between what it was at the start and what it was at the end *may* be significant. By comparison to the initial version, the final product could conceivably be a breakthrough.

The middle category is transformative growth. Some authors use the term breakthrough or disruptive here, with radical as a third category. When disruptive in used, it refers to providing customers with low-cost variations of existing products with incomplete functionality. I've found *transformative* to be a subtly more appropriate descriptor for the middle category as a mid-term link between core and breakthrough products. While some breakthrough products arise suddenly, others may develop through an evolution or slow transformation.

I use the term disruptive growth for the third category to force thinking about significant disruptions to the product category that are long term or future focused. (If you prefer the term *radical*, that's fine.) Whether the product emerges quickly or through step-by-step evolution, the products in this arena differ from the core.

Many companies have used variations of these arenas in explaining business goals for innovation. In 2010, for example, 3M's then CEO George Buckley laid out business goals that mirror these arenas. Protect and strengthen core businesses like abrasives, industrial tapes and optical film (sustaining growth). Develop lower-cost products for emerging markets (transformative growth). Explore future expansion opportunities in areas like renewable energy, water infrastructure and mobile media (disruptive growth).

Harley-Davidson CEO, Jochen Zeitz, announced a new 5-year plan in 2020 dubbed The Hardwire. Similar to the 3M approach, there is a focus on all three arenas.

> Under the new plan, Harley is following a "70-20-10" structure, with 70 percent of its efforts going into the core business, 20 percent into expansion into new segments that offer clear potential for more profit—for instance, the launch of the Pan America adventure bike—and 10 percent on testing ideas for longer-term growth, such as the company's continuing plans to develop small-capacity bikes for new markets in partnership with China's Qianjiang and India's Hero MotoCorp.

In the first book of the ShortRead series, I compared product managers to entrepreneurs. But here is an area I see a nuanced difference. Entrepreneurs often start with a clean sheet without worrying about existing products. As a product manager, you will most likely have a portfolio of both new and existing products. The strategy best suited for your needs will be some combination of offerings in any or all of the three arenas. Start out by asking yourself if you can hit your numbers (i.e., business goals) with your existing products and customers. There is often room for growth; it's a matter of determining the best strategy of *how* to make that happen. The how is incremental product development with line extensions and product marketing.

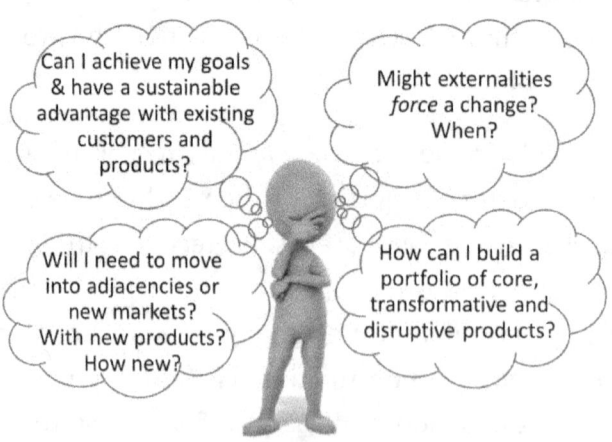

You might not hit your numbers with your core business. If you already own most of the market, if the market is saturated, or if it is edging toward the end of its lifecycle, there may be little room for growth. Or there may be external changes in regulations, competition or customer demands. You may *need* to adapt the products for adjacent markets, or you may *need* to develop new products that are more than line extensions. Or you may need to acquire a product or product line from another company. This middle ground between sustaining and disruptive arenas allows intentional sequencing of growth and development rather than constant incremental reactions.

The final arena is closer to entrepreneurial ventures. Are there trends suggesting that radically different products are necessary for the future? Start exploring. You might not have a product idea for this year, but you are seeding opportunities for tomorrow.

Regardless of which arena(s) you are exploring, you need to evaluate the business potential. How much effort are you going to spend on sustaining core growth, driving transformative growth and seeding opportunities for disruptive growth? Will you spend 70% of your time on core, 20% on transformative and 10% on disruptive? Or will it be 33-33-33? Or 30-20-50? There is no correct answer. It's just important to have a balance of short-term, mid-term and long-term growth goals.

Sustaining Growth

The sustaining growth arena is the foundation of your product strategy. Most of the time, innovation is incremental, building on a base of knowledge that already exists. Core product modifications can yield strong cash flow because of customer connections and brand equity. According to

Apple CEO Tim Cook in 2016, the company had more than a billion devices in use around the world. While industry experts suggest that Apple's new products lack the *wow* factor of the past, the incremental improvements still appeal to its hard-core fan base. So before exploring adjacencies, assess where there is still potential with the core products and extract that potential.

Determine whether you can reposition the same (or a slightly different) products to reach your current customers in new ways. Bayer pain reliever has extended its reach by focusing on specific need areas such as Bayer Back & Body and low-dose versions to prevent heart attacks. Coca Cola's Minute Maid line launched four varieties in 2011: No Pulp 100% Orange Juice, No Pulp 100% Orange Juice with Calcium and Vitamin D, Some Pulp 100% Orange Juice, and Light Orange Juice Beverage with Calcium and Vitamin D.

Sustaining growth or incremental innovation may come from simple changes to the status quo. Can you create a new product by making optional features standard? Or standard features optional? What if you bundled two or more products together? Or broke apart a common bundle? Incremental innovations are a constantly moving target. It's important to keep testing improvements to find those most valuable to customers.

In 2016 Abbott bought heart-device maker St. Jude Medical. According to Industry Week, the move is consistent with Abbott's "track record of generating solid profits in mature markets that other companies have overlooked or exited." CEO Miles White said he welcomed St. Jude's "potential for incremental innovation and growth." It was a recognition of the value that exists in the sustaining growth arena.

Some companies have learned that straying too far from the core too soon can not only increase risks but also cannibalize on strengths. Take Lego for example.

Lego has been an iconic brand for decades. According to [Hubspot](#), Lego was "named *Product of the Century* by [*Fortune Magazine*](#). In 2008, Lego's owner Kjeld Kirk Kristiansen was inducted into the U.S. Toy Industry Hall of Fame." But there have been challenges.

Witness Time Magazine's intriguing headline in 2012: [*Innovation Almost Bankrupted Lego — Until It Rebuilt with a Better Blueprint*](#). According to the article, in 2002 Lego went "on a binge of innovation, adding on Lego-branded electronics, amusement parks, interactive video games, jewelry, education centers and alliances with the *Harry Potter* franchise and the *Star Wars* movies." It even dropped the Duplo brand that year.

Then in 2003, as pointed out by David Robertson in [*Brick by Brick*](#), the company found itself on the brink of bankruptcy. The firm did not defend and extend the core business before branching into adjacencies. The amusement parks drained cash, the theme-licensed products were short-lived, and the diversity added layers of complexity. Many of the products demanded skills that were not part of the Lego business model. Even within the core business, new products competed for retail shelf space with existing products, causing margins to suffer. There were problems with financial controls, supply chains, and cash flow.

Lego went back to the basics. It jettisoned the theme parks and computer business. Then it refocused innovation on the classic Lego blocks. Line extensions and related new products targeted specific niches. Bionicle targeted boys between six and nine years old. Friends targeted girls aged five and up. They relaunched Duplo in 2004.

In 2015, Forbes [nominated Lego](#) as the most powerful brand in the world. According to their 2015 financial report, revenue, profit and margin had increased for each of the prior five years.

What's the take-away for product managers? Don't ignore growth opportunities with your *core* products as you build your product strategy.

You may have one or more top-down (i.e., corporate-driven) goals for your core products, but if not, write your own. Put a stake in the ground, so to speak. The goals can be fiscal-year or multi-year goals or both.

Example goals include revenue and profitability; growth of a specific market segment; cost reallocation; or similar measurable results. For example, a goal could be to grow sales by 25%, generate 15% more online applications, or to increase add-on sales by 30%.

Then determine what you need to do *differently* to move from where you are now to where you want to be (i.e., to attain your stated goals). Note that Lego's goal of returning to profitability included a strategy of retrenchment, cost-cutting, and focused line extensions.

As you plan your strategy for the sustaining growth arena, examine your products. Which are truly core products? Which are most directly linked to your company (or business unit) and customers? Do they need to be changed, or can you improve sales through enhanced marketing efforts? What about products that are not core? Can you eliminate or fine-tune them? (This gets into downstream lifecycle management. While not addressed here, your product strategy, assuming you are a full-stream product manager, will include both new products and management of existing products.)

New products in the sustaining growth arena comprise upgrades to existing products (which may obsolete prior versions), or line extensions (which add new functionality or appeal to specific market segments). These *incremental innovations* can be profitable.

Answer these questions related to your current products.

*Who are the heavy users of your product(s)?

*Is the primary target market growing, stable or declining?

*To which competitors have you lost business, and from which have you gained business? Why?

*Where (in what regions, applications, industries) is competition the strongest? Weakest?

*What is the product life cycle stage? The market life cycle stage?

*What have been trends in terms of unit sales and profitability? Why?

*What changes need to be made?

*What line extensions and upgrades will add value to both the customer and the company?

*What would happen if you made no changes?

*What series of incremental improvements might lead to transformative (or even eventually disruptive) growth in the future?

As you plan extra features, colors, sizes, etc., run financials on both the new product and the related existing product. How much will new products cannibalize current offerings? Will both old and new products continue to be profitable?

Once you have protected the core products and extended them to their logical conclusion, the next part of product strategy is driving growth through adjacent markets and/or adjacent products.

Transformative Growth

Transformative growth comes from looking for opportunities in adjacent product/markets where you can leverage some strengths in your business model. This may include taking your product as is, or tweaking it for different market segments. The classic example is baking soda, a product propelled well beyond baking. Arm & Hammer extended its brand franchise to detergent, toothpaste, and similar products for which the concept of "clean and fresh" was appropriate.

But like any strategic maneuvers, you must manage transformative efforts.

Recall Lego's move into theme parks and electronics products. Some of the growth was transformative, and some was disruptive. Even though many of the end-customers were the same, the rapid influx of new ventures went beyond the standard business model and taxed the ability of the firm to control everything.

Harley-Davidson faced a similar reevaluation of growth approaches. The former CEO had launched a "[More Roads Lead to Harley-Davidson](#)" strategy expanding into all directions simultaneously. The goal was to appeal to non-traditional customers with everything from electric scooters to liquid-cooled sport-bikes. The new CEO changed course to focus on traditional Harley-Davidson customers, including the untapped potential of motivating them to buy new models. New three-wheeled models and the water-cooled Pan America offer transformative growth. As one customer noted, "Lots of H-D owners have pickups and SUVs, and adventure bikes seem to be the pickups and SUVs of the motorcycling world."

Many other companies have moved into adjacent product/markets. For example, years ago the Bendix brake division of Allied Signal increased its brake sales in the do-it-yourself (DIY) market. It discovered that its packaging didn't connote high quality, so it redesigned its packaging to incorporate a strong color blue as part of the repositioning strategy. In one year, its sales moved from less than one percent market share to over 20%.

Consider the changes in capabilities as battery manufacturers redesigned products for toys, hearing aids, cell phones, computers and electric vehicles. Size, power, safety, and compatibility demanded transformative product versions. That even affected supply chains.

Other examples abound. Bike rack manufacturers have moved from car carriers to garage storage to municipal and commercial bike racks. Medical equipment manufacturers have adapted oxygen tanks, beds, mobility equipment and ventilators for home use.

The transformative growth just described happens when growth in the core business is approaching saturation. But since the targeted new customers might require channel or marketing changes, and the non-incremental products can strain manufacturing efficiency, more risk-reduction efforts will need to be part of the strategy.

I suggested earlier that transformative growth can be a stepping stone between incremental and disruptive innovation. Just as some companies have moved too slow to adapt to disruptions, others have moved too fast. One measured approach is to look for hybrid versions of products that connect the old to the new. The Toyota Prius, for example, combined elements from both internal combustion and electric engines. Similarly, MS Office 365 combined cloud and local computing. Nathan Furr and Daniel Snow, in _The Prius Approach_ (Harvard Business Review November 2015), suggest that companies can use hybrids as a stop-gap measure when a disruptive ecosystem is still developing. The hybrid versions are tools for blocking new entrants into the competition, or as a vehicle for learning.

Here are questions to ask yourself about transformative growth.

*What product/markets are adjacent to your core business?

*Do any have growth rates exceeding your existing product/markets?

*How much must you change products to compete?

*Will the new efforts solve internal or external problems, or just be Band-Aids?

*Is there a fit with business strategy and business model?

*How much must you change your business model to compete?

*Can you handle demand if the product is successful?

*Can your channels (if relevant) manage the new inventory?

*What will be your differentiators?

*How loyal are customers to existing products?

*How might *competing* products change to improve customer value, and possibly reduce your advantage?

*How strong are the *companies* producing competing products? Are these products a small percentage of their business or are they main products? What are the companies likely to do if you entered the market? Do you have a plan to deal with that?

*Can you develop a hybrid product to combine elements of core and breakthrough approaches?

*Is the timing right?

*Will you succeed financially?

*Can you win?

Disruptive Growth

The last arena is the disruptive growth arena. This is a long-term strategy that may require changes in your business model. This arena represents a smaller percentage of the product portfolio than the other two. But it will be crucial for the future if ecosystems change.

Coca Cola's move into milk is in the gray area between transformative and disruptive growth. Soft-drink sales fell to a 19-year low in 2013, making it clear why core product growth would be difficult. According to BusinessWeek, "Coke has joined forces with a dairy cooperative to create Fairlife, which produces a filtered, high-protein, low-sugar, lactose-free designer milk also called Fairlife." While the move can take advantage of Coca Cola's marketing expertise and some channel relationships, it demanded collaboration with external partners for the actual product. Fairlife required new competencies beyond those currently in Coca Cola.

Sometimes the disruption comes from something other than the product itself. An example is Gore-Tex, where future growth required disrupting business as usual. Matt Schreiner, Gore-Tex Global Product Specialist, offered this quote on the Outdoor Industry Association website:

> *One of our most significant innovations was the business model we initiated in 1989. Prior to this, we were just selling our laminates and seam tape to the manufacturers; our progress had stopped there. What we learned is that the garments weren't working. While the laminates were working, consumers were getting wet because the garments themselves were suffering from design flaws.*
>
> *In order for us to meet our consumers' expectations, we needed to be more engaged in design thinking and integrate ourselves into the value chain. We worked with our partners*

on design features, such as vents and zippers. We developed and trained an extensive network of factories to our standards. So, we went from a limited view of component performance to a comprehensive view of the whole product.

Today we work collaboratively with our partners on designs and specifications in a trademark license agreement for use of the Gore-Tex trademark. All garments and footwear carrying the Gore-Tex name are manufactured in certified factories, and all designs and components are qualified in our laboratories for waterproof, breathable performance.

Effective product managers plant seeds and gather insights that may disrupt more than the product. In fact, some resulting product concepts may need to be managed separately from the rest of the product category. Apple's electric vehicle project falls into this category. The customers, the technology, the supply chains, and the entire business models are different. While not yet confirming its movement into electric vehicles, Apple has hired a former electric car executive from BMW, leading to speculation of its electric car push.

Scan the horizon for potential game-changers in the industry or in your product category. Prepare for future unknowns. Think beyond your direct competition. The photographic capabilities of cell phones disrupted the camera industry. Digital publishing is changing book publishing strategies. Electronic banking has dramatically affected financial services.

While disruptive growth may be harder to plan for than the other two arenas, it rarely happens so suddenly that no one saw it coming. More likely product managers get caught up in the day-to-day demands of the job, and don't see opportunities until they become crises.

Here are a few questions to ask yourself about disruptive strategy.

*What major changes in your industry have the potential to disrupt your business model now or in the future?

*Can you adapt technologies from other industries or applications to provide novel value in your industry?

*Are there any technologies or processes that might *improve* your efficiency, effectiveness or long-term advantages if you capitalize on them?

*Are there any technologies or processes that might *destroy* your efficiency, effectiveness or long-term advantages if you ignore them?

*Is customer behavior changing in subtle ways that could, over time, result in unique product and service offerings?

*Are there current or proposed laws or requirements that pose opportunities or threats?

*Are there any points in the entire value chain, from supply chain to manufacturing processes to consumption to recycling where you might add value to customers?

Chapter Three: Platform strategy

So far in this ShortRead book I've focused primarily on individual-product strategy. But I would be remiss if I didn't look at strategies that go beyond a single product. This chapter will focus on platforms used for multiple products.

Technology vs. product platforms

There are two very different platforms: digital platforms in technology, and physical platforms in other fields.

A digital platform is an ecosystem designed to enable different groups to co-create value through "plug-and-play" capabilities. The technology infrastructure of the platform touches customers and developers beyond the firm's boundaries. LinkedIn, FaceBook, Google and Amazon—in fact most technology businesses—have platform-based business models.

Physical platforms in other industries refer to product family or product portfolio platforms intended to reduce manufacturing and development costs for new products. Here, a platform is a common architecture, collection of assets, component designs, subsystems, or other elements shared by several products.

The automotive industry exploits shared platforms across various car models. By using the same chassis for different vehicles or using modular sub-systems or common components, companies can improve time-to-market and cost efficiency. Volkswagen, prior to the diesel hit on its reputation and profitability, had designed a mega platform strategy which was considered by many in the industry to be a game-changer. As described several years ago in a Carscoops article:

> Both analysts and the auto industry believe that the MQB could prove to be as revolutionary as Henry Ford's production line or Toyota's "just-in-time" system. VW has been working on it since 2007 and, along with its implementation over the next four years, its investment will reach nearly US$70 billion. Considering that Morgan Stanley estimates it will result in annual gross savings of US$19 billion by 2019, that's money well spent.
>
> Since the MQB is designed for models with a transversely mounted engine, VW also has two other aces up its sleeve: the MLB platform, for models with longitudinally mounted engines, and the MSB, for premium rear- and all-wheel drive models from Porsche, Lamborghini, Bentley and, probably, Audi too.
>
> So that makes three modular platforms, each designed from the outset to use a huge set of common components and be able to accommodate gasoline, diesel and even hybrid powertrains.

Volkswagen has now launched a dedicated MEB platform for electric cars. It applies MQB ideas to "vehicles that are exclusively battery electric."

Over the past decade, other car companies worked toward similar cost-cutting measures. Just Auto suggests that General Motors will follow a plan "to use ten core architectures, many of which will have shared modules, for all future vehicles."

The internet of things is also affecting the car companies. Connectivity is central for many of their growth strategies and they will use global technology platforms besides vehicle platforms.

Both types of platform strategies are important, but the focus in the rest of the chapter will be on product platforms.

Pros and cons of product platforms

There are many benefits to using a product platform strategy: reduce overall costs, force a long-term perspective, and build on customer loyalty.

Use of common components and subsystems can reduce overall, long-term costs and leverage resources to be more efficient and effective. Given that the components and subsystems have already been debugged and tested, the resulting products should have higher quality. Since platform development occurs less frequently than product development, major platform decisions do not need to be made as often. This has the potential to foster lean product development.

Product platforms should "fit" many future products, simplifying future product expansion. This forces a long-term perspective and has the potential to open up diversified revenue streams.

As customers develop preferences for certain platforms, they may become more loyal. This can be especially true in situations where the customer would need to change behavior to use a different platform.

There are potential drawbacks: high upfront costs, risk of platform obsolescence, risk of platform recall affecting many products, and potential duplication of effort.

The upfront costs of platform design and development can be significant. As stated in the Carscoops article, Morgan Stanley estimated the upfront costs of the VW mega platform strategy at $70 billion. Significant savings have to be forecast to justify the investment.

The difference between platform planning beforehand and launching derivatives from an existing platform is one of timing. A platform strategy prescribes the foundational architecture of several future products in advance. The potential risk is that the underlying assumptions were flawed and the foundational approach won't work as planned. And product platforms are not necessarily evergreen. If they become obsolete, the derivative products also risk obsolescence. Product platforms need occasional updating.

There are also quality considerations. If there is a product recall caused by a problem in the platform, a greater number of products will need to be recalled than would be the case without the platform strategy.

Some platforms provide the common architecture for offerings of different product managers. Unless there is strong communication between product managers, there may be duplication of efforts and reduced cost savings.

As with all strategies, product managers have to weigh the positives and the negatives to make the best decision for their product line.

The architecture of product platforms

Geoffrey Moore, in his book *Crossing the Chasm*, discussed the concept of beachhead strategies by using an analogy of Allied soldiers during WWII. He stressed the importance of the troops establishing a beachhead—a foothold or foundation for further advancement—to enable them to dominate the Battle of Normandy. Let's apply the term to product platforms.

A beachhead product platform is a product subsystem for creating functionally different product variants. The product variants may be for different market segments, for good-better-best offerings, or for different usages or applications. Gillette used this strategy with its razors. Its twin-blade strategy spawned Sensor for Men and Sensor for Women. Next, an advanced twin blade platform spawned Sensor-Excel versions for men and women.

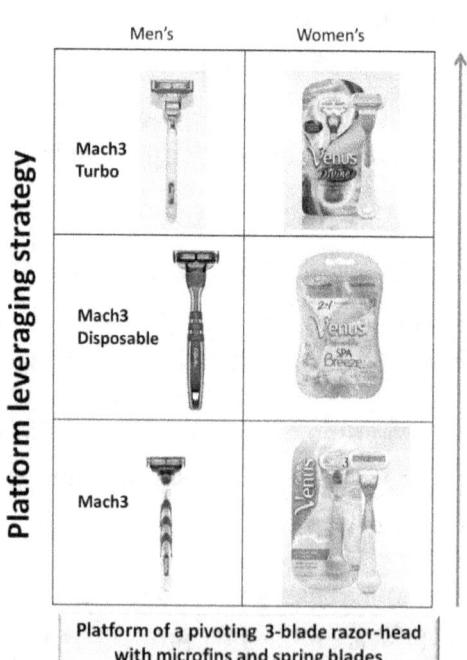

Next it developed a triple blade razor platform, leveraged to the men's Mach3 and the women's Venus (women's Mach3). While the aesthetic designs are different (masculine and feminine), both featured a pivoting head with five microfins and spring blades. The Mach3 blades fit on the Venus razor and vice versa. Disposable versions of the razors ensued. The platform was extended a few years later to include ten microfins (rather than five). The new product variant was the Mach3 Turbo for men and the Venus Divine for women.

A beachhead strategy starts with identifying potential product variants (good-better-best, for example) and market variants (based on demographics, use situations) that have some common elements and some differences. Creating a platform of common elements in advance—like the razor head in the Gillette example—serves as the beachhead and streamlines the development of future products in the family.

In some industries (with highly engineered products) where customization is the norm, platforms may still play a role if you can create a beachhead platform as a starting point. Identify a common platform as a foundation for varied custom products. That would jumpstart the final product, increasing cost efficiency and design effectiveness. If possible, convert the platform into a made-to-stock product to streamline the process even further. This is a basic approach to mass customization, and is benefiting from the mainstreaming of 3D printers.

Another variation of the product platform is the series or franchise platform used in entertainment and publishing. Planning a series of movies (think Star Wars and Harry Potter) in advance—using a platform of themes, characters and sets—builds customer excitement and streamlines the process.

Authors such as Tom Clancy do the same thing. Clancy's multi-book Jack Ryan series (Patriot Games, Hunt for Red October, Clear and Present Danger) used a strong character and setting as the platform. And the series still continues under the authorship of Mark Greaney.

I even designed this book with a platform in mind. I planned a common design upfront to streamline execution. It forced me to map out future products in the series. Then I evaluated the concept by examining customer behavior. Time and attention spans are shorter. People are looking for quick ideas to think about and test. They use mobile devices for more online reading. I determined the upside of using a platform approach overcame any downsides. (I try to use my own advice when I can!)

Companies have propagated product platforms in many directions. Sometimes the process spins off derivative platforms that carry the concept even further.

Here are some questions to ask yourself about product platform opportunities.

- *Are there different market segments or product use situations demanding both common and differentiating product elements?
- *Is there enough commonality to justify a shared platform?
- *Can you design the platform in advance to share across product variants?
- *Will the upfront time, effort and cost allow streamlined processes or reduced total costs?
- *Will the future products have a competitive advantage? Will customers care?

*Do you have the expertise required for future products in the family?

*Will you need new technology to turn future product ideas into a reality? When will that technology be available?

*What are the potential negatives to using a platform approach? Is the upside potential greater than the downside risk?

*Can you test several plausible platforms?

*Can you use platforms in some situations and stand-alone products in others?

*Are there any cases where derivative platforms could streamline your product group?

Chapter Four: Roadmapping

Roadmap is another term used in several ways. Many software companies use it to define the timing of future releases. Some companies use it as a project tool for product development. Most use it from a more strategic perspective.

There are roadmap variations for different purposes. *Industry roadmaps* promote ongoing collaboration and alignment among companies to address industry-wide concerns. They often contain regulatory and technology forecasts.

Technology roadmaps may be industry wide, applying to many companies. In other situations, individual companies develop them as part of R&D planning. These roadmaps capture capabilities and timing of plausible quantum leaps. They also provide input into make-versus-buy decisions.

Market opportunity roadmaps provide a future timeline for a company's planned moves into adjacent or new markets, linking to corporate strategy. They specify the sequencing of market growth.

Product or platform roadmaps are planning tools for product management. They project the expected launches of future products during the execution of strategy.

Comprehensive roadmapping involves compiling a consensus view of the future landscape across all these dimensions, along with the timeline-based evolution of products and technologies that get you there. Most companies have a hodgepodge of roadmaps (or plans) that are not well-connected. When several roadmaps align strategically, the result is an integrated roadmap or timeline, as shown in the following figure.

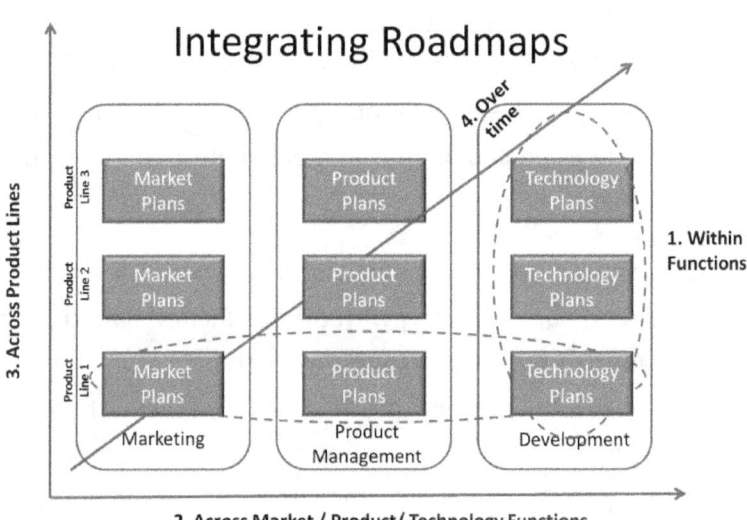

Source: SIMposium08" "Enterprise Roadmapping"

Note that there are plans (roadmaps) within functions, across functions, across product lines, and over time. At the top level, an integrated roadmap is visionary, directional and an umbrella over functions and product lines. It likely looks out 2-5 years, with an annual update. The product roadmap may be longer or shorter, but coexists with the top-level roadmap.

Envision a Collectively Identified Future

The value of the process lies in forcing individuals to articulate their assumptions and in integrating information. As a result, it encourages consensus, contributes to better forecasting, and provides a framework for thinking about the future. The process may uncover promising new technologies, "repurpose" parts from different products and designs, and/or help align technology roadmaps with suppliers. Motorola, for example, tries to select components and suppliers *before* design takes place. By developing multiyear technology roadmaps, Motorola can source suppliers with the needed capabilities and willingness to invest in technology alignment.

A product roadmap is a document that a product manager drafts in collaboration (directly or indirectly) with other functional areas. It describes a collectively identified future environment, with high-level initiatives to move toward that future. The document brings together company strategy, market data, technological growth trajectories, and product family plans. The goal is not only to capitalize on environmental turning points as soon as possible but also to integrate technology and resources across products and/or product lines.

A product roadmap is not a project plan

What I just described is a document that is a tool to communicate high-level strategy to alliance partners, analysts, management, and sometimes key customers. Given the vast audience that may be privy to this roadmap, it includes snippets of other plans in the company. But it does not contain confidential data.

The product roadmap is a business plan for the product owner (i.e., the product manager). It contains probable scenarios based on current expectations, forecasts and assumptions. The objective is to aid in the product line's growth. The product roadmap is not a project plan, but a strategy, business planning, and communication tool.

CREATING THE ROADMAP

Roadmapping may start at a meeting (or workshop) whereby technology, market and product experts meet to evaluate a preliminary matrix of product and platform goals for the product family. Integrating all these variables is a moving target, requiring iteration (and finesse). The chronological sequencing of components is agreed to first in terms of roadmap goals. Then timing is added on the product family roadmap.

Roadmap Goals

		Segment A	Segment B	Segment C
New product		Stand-alone product (Clara)		New product for Segment B based on common beachhead platform LoKo-B	Stand-alone product for Segment C (HomeSite)
Best		Good, better, best from product platform AKM-3			Better & best Segment C products from beachhead platform LoKo-C3
Better		AKM-2		Good & better products from beachhead platform LoKo-A2	LoKo-C2
Good		AKM-1		LoKo-A1	
		Product platform (AKM)		Beachhead platform (LoKo)	

In the example roadmap goals matrix, there are two proposed platforms and two proposed stand-alone products. The platform in the left column is a product-only platform, with no market segment variations. It will have different value configurations (AKM-1, AKM-2 and AKM-3) of good, better and best offerings. The second is a beachhead platform (LoKo) with both vertical (markets A, B and C) and horizontal (product use/quality) configurations, similar to the earlier Gillette example. The LoKo platform should spawn five derivative products: LoKo-A1, LoKo-A2, LoKo-B, LoKo-C2 and LoKo-C3. There are goals for two stand-alone products (Clara and HomeSite).

During the meeting, the individuals will assess the viability of the platforms and the fit of the platforms for the intended derivative products. Then they will hash out time frames. This is an iterative process during which they will change the initial matrix, with subtly new goals and directions. After several iterations, they'll finish a new matrix with revised goals for the product family.

Product Family Roadmap											
2022				2023				2024			
Q1	Q2	Q3	Q4	Q1	Q2	Q3	Q4	Q1	Q2	Q3	Q4
Platform AKA Complete			AKM1		AKM2		AKM3				
		Platform LoKo complete		LoKo-A1		LoKo-A2	LoKo-C2	LoKo-C3			LoKo-B
	HomeSite							Clara			

Then they will re-examine time frames. This step will look more like the traditional technology roadmaps. There may be a master roadmap for the entire product family along with roadmaps for each platform, and perhaps the platform and derivatives. If multiple platforms are to be used with multiple products, such as in the automotive industry, pulling everything together on a single roadmap will be challenging. In those situations, logic dictates that the platform roadmap be separate from the future products. The following roadmap takes the prior platform and stand-alone goals and adds time frames.

It's important to remember that this is a learning process. Just as a geographic map to reach your vacation destination won't uncover all road construction and accidents, a product roadmap won't foresee every setback. Adjustments will be inevitable. Platform concepts, derivatives, and/or stand-alone products may require modifications.

So here are some questions to ask yourself about your roadmapping process.

*Have you taken a broad look at internal variables—even beyond your area of control—as part of your product strategy and planning processes?

*Did you use a collaborative, data-driven approach?

*Do you view your roadmap as a strategy tool or as a project management document?

*Is it a static or dynamic document?

*Does your roadmap address your entire product family, including stand-alone products, platforms and derivative products?

Chapter Five: Product market research

The title of this book is Product Strategies and Roadmaps. You'd expect the content to cover planning for products. But the true value of products comes from customers and what they're willing to pay for. Customer knowledge, awareness of product markets, provides the foundation for everything else. This chapters dives into the research to make it happen.

THE RESEARCH PYRAMID

Product managers use research and data to inform decision making. They strive to know what has happened in their product markets, why it happened, and what might happen next. That's core of the analytics pyramid from hindsight to insight to foresight.

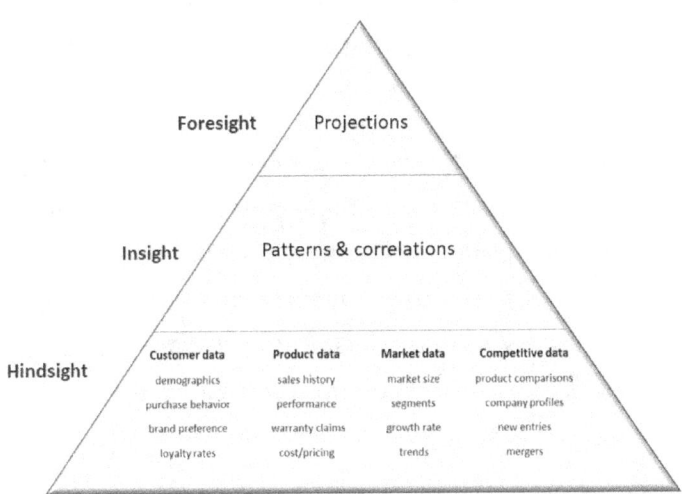

Hindsight is the review of past and present data that is primarily descriptive. It's the collection of facts and statistics, such as sales history, purchase behavior, product performance and satisfaction ratings. Hindsight answers the question: what happened?

Insight is the investigation of patterns that help explain the reason things happened the way they did. It could involve attempting to explain shifts in trend lines, or how one variable (say price or advertising) affects another (perhaps sales). Insight answers the question: why are things happening the way they are, and why did things happen that way in the past?

Foresight is the theorization of the future. It is the effort to determine the likelihood of a coming event or specific situation. It may involve mathematical (predictive) modeling or "best guess" hypotheses. Foresight tries to answer the question: what might happen in the future?

Foresight is sometimes "fuzzy" and requires you to be creative. Step back and redefine the business in terms of customer functions. When David

Whitman became CEO of Whirlpool, his vision was to transform the company into a customer-focused organization. He wanted to shift thinking from product to customer, as stated in the following excerpt from an interview in Harvard Business Review:

> The starting point isn't the existing product; it's the function consumers buy products to accomplish. When you return to first principles, the design issues dramatically change. The microwave couldn't have been invented by someone who assumed he or she was in the business of designing a range. Such a design breakthrough required seeing the opportunity is "easier, quicker food preparation," not "a better range."
>
> Take the "fabric-care business," which we used to call the "washing-machine business." We're now studying consumer behavior from the time people take off their dirty clothes at night until they've been cleaned and ironed and hung in the closet. What are we looking for? The worst part of the process is not the washing and drying. The hard part is when you take your clothes out of the dryer and you have to do something with them—iron, fold, hang them up. Whoever comes up with a product to make this part of the process easier, simpler, or quicker is going to create an incredible market.

The Analytics Pyramid Questions

Hindsight
- What happened?
- Descriptive data

Insight
- Why did it happen?
- Diagnostic data

Foresight
- What might happen?
- Predictive data

There is no one research approach that applies exclusively to one stage of analytics. Averages, percentages and totals from quantitative tools may be descriptive. Or you might analyze them to identify patterns and correlations. Similarly, qualitative techniques such as focus groups and case studies may help understand what is happening today, but may also shed light on what might happen tomorrow.

COMMON RESEARCH DICHOTOMIES

Product market research is the gathering, recording, and analysis of details relevant to a business decision. The data are inputs into hindsight, insight, or foresight. Tweaking studies, using diverse techniques, or applying layered methods can yield improved results. Depending on time, budget, and other resources, a combination of approaches will almost always provide better answers than one approach.

Let's start with different dichotomies that are common. The endpoints of each dichotomous scale have differing advantages and disadvantages that a product manager should weigh in deciding on the best approach to use.

Quantitative versus qualitative is one of the most common distinctions. Quantitative studies typically require large—and most often probability—samples that enable statistical analysis. Qualitative studies have fewer participants and facilitate a deeper understanding of a topic. If you desire results that are replicable and scalable, you will need to lean quantitative. If you want to dig into something obscure and without clear parameters, qualitative is the way to go.

Investigators commission primary research for their own use. This allows the researchers to probe specifically into a focus area. Secondary research is the examination of results published by someone else for another purpose. While the intended purpose is different, it may unearth ideas you overlooked, or help shape your primary research.

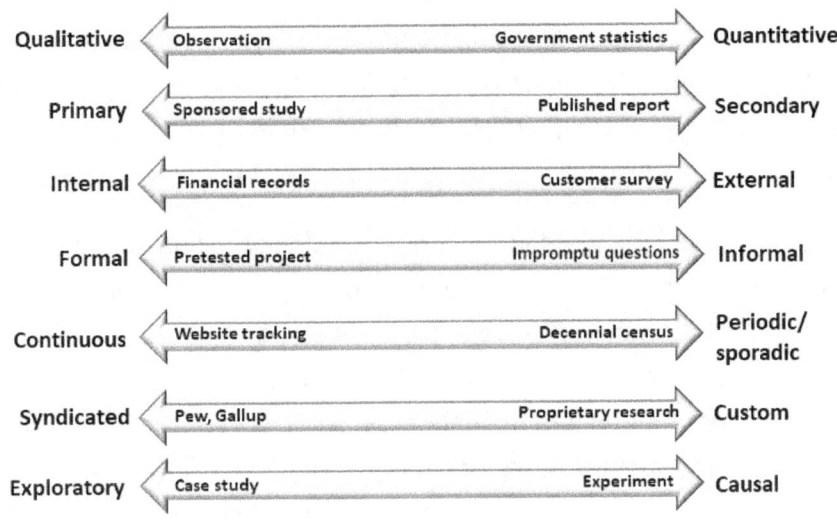

Internal fact-finding applies sources, such as financial records, housed within a business or institution. Some records are unavailable any other way. External fact-finding goes beyond the organization's walls.

Formal inquiries require the careful planning and execution of a prescribed project. Informal inquiries yield understanding from, for example, impromptu questions asked by a customer service representative. While formal inquiries are more carefully controlled, informal inquiries can trigger new perspectives.

Continuous data collection is ongoing and systematic, often with the help of technology. Website tracking provides reams of data for hindsight, but requires further analysis for insight or foresight. Periodic or sporadic data collection occurs at prescribed intervals or as needed. Sometimes focused data collection can aid researchers in interpreting continuous data.

Syndicated investigations refer to projects that are independently conducted, investigated and sold by firms such as Pew and Gallup. Since these firms employ experts and have more resources than many individual firms, the results are more statistically concrete. Custom investigations are proprietary and applied to a narrower issue. Whether a survey, user testing, or case study, custom investigations provide a more laser-focused approach.

Exploratory analyses look for ideas and insights, along the line of a private eye attempting to ferret out hidden secrets. Focus groups, in-depth interviews, and case studies provide a learn-as-you-go experience. Causal analyses are confirmatory, striving to identify cause-and-effect relationships. Experimental design analyses, with managed experimental and control groups, pinpoint the effect of one thing on something else. Unfortunately, they shed little light on variables outside the control of the analysis.

Tools, Methods and Techniques

As is clear from the prior section, tools and methods fit beyond one dichotomy, or one analytics question. A focus group is exploratory when used to understand what happened. It helps with hindsight. However, it might also interpret quantitative results that are perplexing. In that case it becomes a tool for insight. And if the focus group comprises industry experts discussing trends, the output is useful for foresight.

What I want you to take away from the discussion is the need to first think about the decision you are making, and secondly to think about tools and techniques. But when you do so, use a broad net.

To help with that goal, I'm presenting several tools, methods and techniques for you to consider in your product strategy journey.

Secondary research. This refers to data collected by someone other than the primary user. Industry reports, government statistics, and prepackaged market research are all examples. I advise starting with secondary research for several reasons. First, you don't want to reinvent the wheel; it's possible that the question you are asking has already been answered. Second, the content, phrasing, or categories in secondary sources may help refine a necessary primary study. Third, statistics in terms of market size (applicable to forecasting product sales) may be unavailable through other sources. The vision statements presented earlier all relied on a healthy dose of secondary research. But there may be downsides. Always evaluate the potential for bias in secondary data. Who published it? Why was it published? Was the methodology sound?

Focus group. This is research in a group setting. Six to twelve people share their opinions on a topic. While traditionally conducted face-to-face, technology has fostered virtual focus groups. Successful groups encourage members to talk with each other rather than simply answer questions from the moderator. This causes a snowball effect of gathering fresh ideas. Focus groups are useful for product ideation, concept testing, and many exploratory and qualitative goals.

Survey. This is a research method that can fit across the board. It can be qualitative or quantitative, formal or informal, internal or external, or somewhere in between. Surveys use questionnaires given to select samples. The size and randomness of the sample dictate whether statistical analysis is possible. Questionnaire design and pretesting are critical for unbiased results. Question wording must be unambiguous. Response categories must be appropriate for the type of analysis desired. Open-ended questions are useful for gathering ideas you might have overlooked. Scaled responses might be necessary for statistical analysis (chi square, regression). Web surveys are increasingly common and can be useful. Just don't expect them to provide quantitative, statistical, probabilistic, replicable results.

<u>Ethnography</u>. Also known as observational research, ethnography means going out into your customer's world and "walking in their shoes." Your goal is to see how customers use, enjoy, adapt to, and/or struggle with a product or service. It's possible that customers may not even be aware of their own behavior and therefore cannot verbally suggest product improvements. Customer visit programs are a form of ethnographic research to spot product gaps, needs, or opportunities. Findings might generate simple product modifications, or even innovative breakthroughs.

While the insights you glean from *users* occasionally prompts breakthrough ideas, it's more likely *non-user ethnography* will be appropriate. How do people *not* using the product category get the job done without the product? How much would you need to adapt your products to be successful in these adjacent markets?

<u>Lead user research</u>. Professor Eric von Hippel from the MIT Sloan School of Management championed this method. It focuses on gathering ideas from people or industries that are already solving problems you are grappling with. For example, von Hippel explained how the automotive industry learned several ideas for antilock brakes from the aerospace industry. Similarly, <u>Nike adapted the seat foam created by NASA</u> for use as a lightweight foam (Lunarlon) for shoes. And Carestream Dental adapted <u>Northrop Grumman's technology</u> for detecting structural aerospace defects to the medical industry. Its LOGICON software with sensors helps dentists to more clearly identify tooth cavities.

I've worked with product managers in the CPG food industry who used chefs as lead users to identify trends in food preferences. And I've met industrial product managers who interacted with individuals at <u>Maker Faires</u>

to think differently about the product. These approaches involve collaboration with well-qualified experts and possibly progressive customers who—compared with "mainstream" customers—can offer more unconventional concepts. It's clear that lead users could identify unique solutions to problems with existing products, but also the potential for transformative and breakthrough products.

Competitive comparisons. Understanding the competition vis-à-vis your product is an absolute strategy sine qua non. Not only should you compare your product and its features against competition, you also need to attain customer perspective on those issues. Which markets and which segments prefer your product and/or features? And why? Some research can be ongoing through online analysis tools, at least for situations when keywords and searches are common. Competitive comparisons don't stop at features. Mergers, acquisitions, and product strategy changes can influence the future success of your product.

Minimum viable product. MVP is a concept that bridges research and new product development. It's the process of developing a product with sufficient functionality to gain customer insight about its business viability. It's part of a strategy of experimentation, iteration and agility. While most commonly applied to digital products (which don't require expensive tooling or machining to establish a basic version of a final product), there are some workarounds for manufactured products. Companies are using product simulations or rapid prototyping with 3-D printers to have a demonstrable product for gathering customer feedback (besides proof of concept).

Cross-industry intelligence. This refers to exploring outside the company or industry for new ideas. Rather than adapting a product, component, or material to a product category, this may involve adapting a business model or process knowledge. Ramon Vullings and Marc Heleven, in Not Invented Here: Cross-Industry Innovation, encourage people to go beyond best practices to next practices by fusing, blending, adapting and experimenting with ideas from other industries. According to the authors, food, boating and car companies adapted the Airbnb business model in their industries. They also pointed out that the model for BMW's iDrive design was the video-game industry.

Boundless listening™. This isn't actually a research method, but it's my term for an approach related to insight and foresight. It's about the job of being a product manager. It means embracing open-mindedness to expand your mental network. Have brown-bag lunches with R&D. Encourage sales force input on product modifications and replacements. Build touch points with customer service. Engage supply chain partners in mutual exploration of better materials, processes, and efficiencies. Break down customer requests to look for potential platform ideas for other customer products. Listen to perspectives and approaches different from yours before tying yourself to one worldview. Boundless listening is just what it sounds like—being fully open to hearing new ideas from virtually any sources.

Chapter Six: Self-reflection

Rate each of these statements on a 1-5 scale, with 1 being "always," 3 being "sometimes" and 5 being "never." The more often you answer 1 or 2 to these questions, the stronger is your aptitude for product management.

How often do you...

12345	Elevate your product thinking beyond "business as usual?"
12345	Define specific goals toward which you build your product strategy?
12345	Include inspirational benefits in the product vision?
12345	Ensure your product concepts fit your vision?
12345	Scrutinize a first-to-market strategy as a possible—rather than a definite—approach?
12345	Consider potential changes in customer behavior to determine whether your new product is likely to be an easy sell, a smash hit, a long-haul, or a sure failure?
12345	Revise your plan to defend and extend your core products? To drive growth in adjacent opportunities? To seed options for future growth?
12345	Make your differentiators crystal clear?
12345	Maintain objectivity about what it takes to win?

1 2 3 4 5	Incorporate cross-functional plans on market, product and technology?
1 2 3 4 5	Include stand-alone products, platforms and future derivatives in your roadmap?
1 2 3 4 5	Employ hindsight, insight, AND foresight?
1 2 3 4 5	Test new research approaches to generate new growth options?
1 2 3 4 5	Evaluate your product strategy from both a customer and a business case perspective?

SUGGESTED REFERENCES

Product Vision

There are many approaches to product vision, but all recognize the importance of understanding customers. *Build What Matters*, while leaning toward software companies, focuses on frameworks to gain a deep understanding of the customer definition of success. Vivid Vision, while geared toward company visions, emphasizes the importance of a shared view of the future.

*Build What Matters: Delivering Key Outcomes with Vision-Led Product Management by Ben Foster and Rajesh Nerlikar

*Vivid Vision: A Remarkable Tool For Aligning Your Business Around a Shared Vision of the Future by Cameron Herold

Growth Strategies

Growth can come from getting more money from your core products, or from innovating breakthroughs. Product managers should have knowledge of both. Two "classic" books are *Profit from the Core* (stressing value from existing products), and *Crossing the Chasm* (focusing on the diffusion of innovation). The concepts are valid even if the books are now a bit dated. *Upstream Marketing* delves into the fuzzy front end of product strategy. *Compete Smarter* addresses strategic thinking to set priorities. *Create the Future* incorporates trend watching into the strategy of growth.

*Profit from the Core: A Return to Growth in Turbulent Times by Chris Zook and James Allen

*Crossing the Chasm: Marketing and Selling High-Tech Products to Mainstream Customers by Geoffrey Moore

*Upstream Marketing: Unlock Growth Using the Combined Principles of Insight, Identity, and Innovation by Tim Koelzer and Kristin Kurth

*Compete Smarter, Not Harder: A Process for Developing the Right Priorities Through Strategic Thinking by William Putsis

*Create the Future + the Innovation Handbook: Tactics for Disruptive Thinking by Jeremy Gutsche

Product Platforms and Roadmaps

While companies often view new product development from the lens of individual products, the importance of platforms is clear. Alvin Lehnerd and Marc Meyer, in *The Power of Product Platforms*, explain how to design product platforms, using examples from Black & Decker, Hewlett-Packard and others. Most other books cover *technology* platforms and roadmaps, although it is useful information for other products. Some that fall into this category are *Product Roadmaps Relaunched* and *Product Direction*.

*The Power of Product Platforms: Building Value and Cost Leadership by Alvin P. Lehnerd and Marc H. Meyer

*Product Roadmaps Relaunched: How to Set Direction while Embracing Uncertainty by C. Todd Lombardo, Bruce McCarthy, Evan Ryan, and Michael Connors

*Product Direction: How to build successful products at scale with Strategy, Roadmaps, and Objectives and Key Results (OKRs) by Nacho Bassino

Product Market Research

There are tried-and-true marketing research techniques and contemporary technological adaptations. Both play a role. I recommend starting with the basics to learn how to control for bias in communication and process. *The Marketing Research Toolbox* is useful in that regard. *User Research* highlights the more common approaches of UX designers, with some carryover for other products.

*The Market Research Toolbox: A Concise Guide for Beginners by Edward F. (Francis) McQuarrie

*User Research: A Practical Guide to Designing Better Products and Services by Stephanie Marsh

About the Author

Linda Gorchels

Linda Gorchels is a School of Business emeritus from the University of Wisconsin-Madison. During her time at the university, she worked in what is now the Center for Executive and Professional Development, training over 10,000 corporate executives from the United States and globally. Author of numerous books, she has also written for many trade magazines and academic journals. Her books have been translated into multiple languages. Life-long learning remains her passion, and she is dedicated to sharing that passion with others.

Books in the ShortRead Series

This is a series for those involved in developing products and services. While the emphasis started with product management, some topics (like creativity) span many disciplines.

Product managers, like other business people, want bite-sized learning. They want to dive into a topic without swimming across the whole lake at one time. The ShortRead Series allows readers to space out learning, to focus on specific content. Studies have proven this approach helps learners absorb and remember more. You can decide to follow the links in the series to go deeper, or skim the various topics one at a time. Depth versus breadth or both is your choice.

PRODUCT MANAGEMENT 101

Product Management 101 is a pragmatic resource to grasp, refine, and master this comprehensive job function.

Written 25 years after publication of the first edition of *The Product Manager's Handbook* (now in its 4th edition), it *examines the past, present and future of product management.*

Crammed with tips, links, and resources, it helps you advance your career. Do you know how to overcome confirmation bias in your decision making? Can you apply proper business acumen? Are you able to influence people over whom you have no authority? How close are you to being a T-Shaped individual, and why should you care? Product Management 101 helps answer these questions and more.

The book:

> ***Provides an overview for novices***. Basic role definitions. Job descriptions and metrics. Required competencies. High-level how-to strategies.
>
> ***Fills gaps for mid-level product managers***. Most don't have formal training for the position. This book closes the voids.
>
> ***Gut-checks job performance for pros***. Just as sports pros maintain command of nitty-gritty basics, expert product managers acknowledge the value of revisiting foundational skills.

Regardless of your experience level, the last chapter invites you to self-assess. Use the information to hone your strengths and shore up your weaknesses.

PRODUCT STRATEGY & ROADMAPS

Are you a strategic thinker? Or do you find it hard to rise above the fray of day-to-day thinking?

Product Strategy & Roadmaps can help you move from operational to strategic thinking. It starts with foundational definitions. Next, it provides succinct and structured guidance on writing vision statements. It puts context into evaluating growth arenas. Then it shows how to integrate these thought processes into crafting product strategy and roadmaps.

The book addresses questions such as:

> What does product strategy include?
>
> Is there a difference between a product vision and a product concept?
>
> Under what circumstances should you be first to market?

What are the three growth arenas and how much effort should you allocate to each?

How should you approach creating a product family roadmap?

What are the pros and cons of product platforms?

Will better customer research improve your hindsight, insight and foresight?

Product Strategy & Roadmaps provides a disciplined, yet flexible way for product managers to plan for the future.

Books by this Author

THE PRODUCT MANAGER'S HANDBOOK

The Product Manager's Handbook was a prototypical resource book for product management. It was one of the first to overview this comprehensive field. Now in its fourth edition, it shows you how to integrate your organization's disparate segments into a cooperative, results-focused unit that produces satisfying products—from initial design through the post-purchase experience.

PRODUCT MANAGEMENT 101

Product Management 101 is a pragmatic resource to grasp, refine, and master this comprehensive job function.

Written 25 years after publication of the first edition of *The Product Manager's Handbook* (now in its 4th edition), it *examines the past, present and future of product management.*

Crammed with tips, links, and resources, it helps you advance your career. Do you know how to overcome confirmation bias in your decision making? Can you apply proper business acumen? Are you able to influence people over whom you have no authority? How close are you to being a T-Shaped individual, and why should you care? Product Management 101 helps answer these questions and more.

The book:

> **Provides an overview for novices**. Basic role definitions. Job descriptions and metrics. Required competencies. High-level how-to strategies.
>
> **Fills gaps for mid-level product managers**. Most don't have formal training for the position. This book closes the voids.

Gut-checks job performance for pros. Just as sports pros maintain command of nitty-gritty basics, expert product managers acknowledge the value of revisiting foundational skills.

Regardless of your experience level, the last chapter invites you to self-assess. Use the information to hone your strengths and shore up your weaknesses.

THE MANAGER'S GUIDE TO DISTRIBUTION CHANNELS

Channel management is an important component of a firm's competitive strategy. Mistakes can cost companies million. **The Manager's Guide to Distribution Channels** provides managers and decision makers with proven tools and go-to-market strategies for refining channel strategies and managing distribution relationships. Self-assessment tools combine with real-world cases and examples to give managers a non-theoretical, balanced blend of thought-provoking insights and hands-on tactics. The publication of the book preceded the growth of internet channels, but remains a resource for the movement of physical products from manufacture to customer.

BUSINESS MODEL RENEWAL

Forget "business as usual."
Don't believe everything you read about "best practices."
There is no "magic bullet."

Markets are continually changing. Perhaps you must renew your business model.

Business Model Renewal provides a language and multiple frameworks for how to think about and implement business model reinvention.

www.ingramcontent.com/pod-product-compliance
Lightning Source LLC
Chambersburg PA
CBHW070457220526
45466CB00004B/1856